MOUNTAINS

Angela Wilkes

Illustrated by Peter Dennis

Revised by Felicity Brooks and Stephen Wright

Contents

Consultant: Edward Bates
Senior Lecturer
Whitelands College, Roehampton
Institute of Higher Education

In the Mountains

High mountains are always cold, even in summer. And the higher you go, the colder it is. Often the snowy peaks are hidden by clouds.

A group or row of mountains is called a mountain range.

Eagle

It is too cold for trees to grow above a certain height on mountains. This height is called the tree-line.

Only evergreen trees grow high on mountains. They have tough, needle-like leaves which help them to stay alive through the winters.

Mountain goats

The top of a mountain is called the summit or peak.

The height above which there is snow all the year round on a mountain is called the snow-line.

A narrow gap between two mountains is called a pass.

Winds blowing from one direction have stunted and bent this tree.

Above the tree-line the ground is mostly rocky and bare. Some plants grow between the rocks, where they are sheltered from the cold winds.

Mountain flowers are small and have long roots to help them find water. They grow and flower in the spring and summer when it is warm.

3

Living in the Mountains

People in the past often moved from the coasts and plains to escape invaders. They settled in the mountains. In Peru they built high fortress towns which they could defend from attack.

Mountain houses have thick walls to keep out the cold. In the Himalayas the animals live on the ground floor and the people live upstairs.

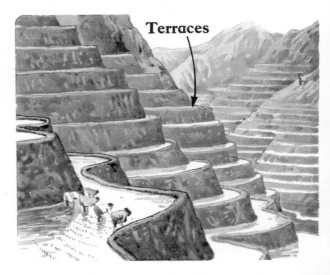

Terraces

It is hard to grow food on steep slopes. In the Philippines, farmers built terraces round the mountains and planted rice on the narrow steps.

Llamas

Mountain people are tough and can stand the cold. They carry huge loads on their backs.

They have few farm tools or machines. These women in the Himalayas are digging up potatoes.

People in Peru keep llamas. They carry heavy loads and their dung is used as fuel.

Women in the Andes weave their clothes from llama wool. They sell the brightly-coloured cloth at village markets.

Monks have built many monasteries in mountains. They thought that the nearer they were to the sky, the nearer they were to their gods.

5

Travelling in the Mountains

Yak

In the Himalayas there are few roads. Yaks carry loads along narrow tracks.

Strong porters carry baggage when the track is too steep and dangerous for yaks.

In some countries, where mountains are too steep to drive up, zig-zag roads have been built.

Crossing mountain rivers has always been difficult. Many are in deep gorges. In the Himalayas and Andes you can still see rope bridges.

These kind of bridges were first built hundreds of years ago. Crossing them is quite difficult because they sway easily.

Cable car

Cable cars carry people and stores up mountains at ski resorts. Cabins on cables are wound up and down between the stations at each end.

Mountain railways need many tunnels and bridges. The Rhaetian railway in Switzerland has 376 bridges and 76 tunnels in 240 km.

The Pilatus line in Switzerland is one of the world's steepest railways. The engine turns a toothed wheel in a toothed rail to drive it uphill.

Wild Animals

These brown bears live in the forests on the lower slopes of the Rockies. They are big but are gentle unless hungry or scared.

Bears eat all kinds of food – berries, roots, insects and meat. They sharpen their long claws by scratching at the bark of trees.

Young bears are playful and can climb trees. They look for honey in wild bees' nests.

Brown bears are good at catching fish. They flip them out of the water with their paws.

Bears spend the winter asleep in dens. They dig deep holes in the ground or find dry caves.

Hunters

Timber wolf

Timber wolves still roam mountain forests in North America. They hunt in packs, running very fast to catch and kill animals.

Pumas live in the Rockies and go hunting in the daytime. They creep up silently on quite big animals, then leap on them and eat them.

The hunted

Snowshoe hare

Porcupine

Alpine marmot

Snowshoe hares grow white coats in winter. This makes it hard for attackers to see them.

When the porcupine is in danger, its quills stand up and stick into anything they touch.

If danger is near, an Alpine marmot whistles to warn other marmots to dive into their burrows.

In a Swiss Valley

In Switzerland most mountain people live in the valleys, where there is good farmland.

This stream comes from melted snow high on the mountain.

Farmland

Hut where hay is kept

It is late summer in this valley in the Alps. The farmers are cutting the long grass and stacking it so that it will dry into hay.

When the winter comes, they will feed it to their cows, which are kept inside until the spring. Some cow's milk is made into butter and cheese.

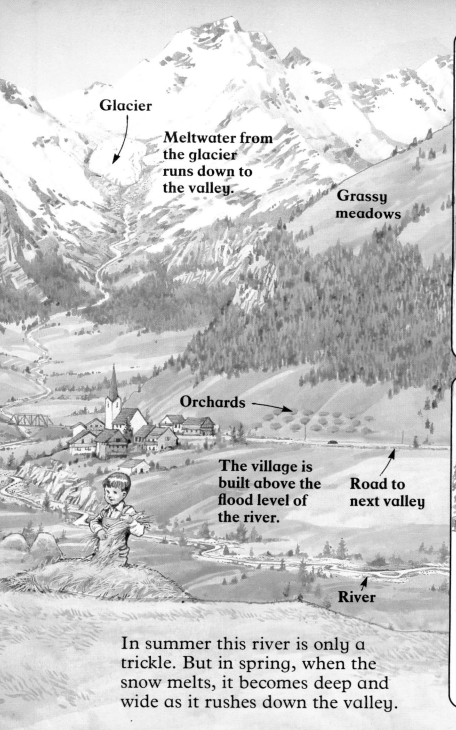

Glacier

Meltwater from the glacier runs down to the valley.

Grassy meadows

Orchards →

The village is built above the flood level of the river.

Road to next valley

← **River**

In summer this river is only a trickle. But in spring, when the snow melts, it becomes deep and wide as it rushes down the valley.

In the summer the cows are taken up to graze in meadows above the tree-line.

The village houses are built of wood and stone. They are called chalets.

Above the Tree-line

High in the mountains there are bare, rocky slopes and cliffs.

It is too cold and windy for trees and most plants to grow there.

Eagle's nest

Golden eagle

These mountain goats live high in the Rockies, where they are safe from attackers. They have thick, shaggy coats to keep them warm.

They jump nimbly from ledge to ledge, looking for plants to eat. Special pads on their hoofs stop them from slipping on the rocks.

The golden eagle glides high in the sky, searching for small animals. When it sees one, it swoops down and catches it in its claws.

The rare snow leopard lives in high, cold parts of the Himalayas. It sleeps in a rocky den during the day and hunts small animals at night.

Mountain flowers grow under the snow. The edelweiss's fuzzy petals may help keep it warm.

Like most mountain flowers, the blue poppy flowers in the spring, when the snow melts.

This flower grows in cracks in the rock. It grows fluff around its petals to keep it warm.

Above the Clouds

High mountain peaks are covered in ice and snow all the year round. Nothing can grow there. Under the ice and snow there is only rock.

The peaks are sharp and jagged. Ice and frost split the rock so that bits of it break off and the shapes of the peaks slowly change.

Griffon vulture

The wind is very strong at the top of a mountain. It blows the snow into strange shapes, or blows it away to show patches of bare rock.

One of the few signs of life high in the Himalayas are huge griffon vultures. They soar above the snow, looking for dead animals to eat.

The tops of mountains are often in sunshine above the clouds. But there is always the danger of bad weather and snowstorms.

Sometimes a mountaineer sees a strange shape, like a ghost, on the clouds below him. This is really a huge shadow of himself.

Climbing the Peaks

Goggles

It is cold high in the mountains. Climbers always wear warm clothes and thick boots.

They also wear goggles, because the sun and the glare from the snow could make them blind.

They clip spikes on to their boots. These help give them a firm foothold on slippery ice.

Ice axe

Oxygen mask

Climbers always rope themselves together. Each one also ties the rope to an ice axe which can be jammed into the snow if one of them slips.

There is very little air to breathe on high mountains. Climbers carry oxygen tanks on their backs and breathe the oxygen through masks.

Winter Sports

Cable car

Skiers zig-zag down slopes so they do not go too fast.

This skier is jumping over a steep ridge.

Ski resort

Cross-country skiers

Ski school

In the winter, when the snow is deep, people go to the mountains for skiing holidays. Special resorts have been built for them.

People are taught to ski on gentle slopes. When they are good enough, they ski down steeper ones. Cable cars take them to the mountain tops.

Avalanche!

An avalanche starts when a huge slab of snow begins to slide down a mountain. It may be set off by people walking on a slope.

An avalanche causes a huge rush of wind. The wind alone blew this coach off a mountain bridge. The snow itself did not reach the bridge.

Avalanches often start after a heavy snowfall, or in the spring when the snow begins to melt. This is an avalanche of powdery snow.

Moving faster and faster, it crashes downhill into the valley. It uproots trees and crushes or buries any houses in its way.

After an avalanche, rescue teams prod the snow to find people who have been buried in it.

Trained dogs sniff for people under the snow. If they are found quickly, they may still be alive.

Injured people are put on special stretchers. Helicopters carry them to the nearest hospital.

Roofs built over roads protect cars from the snow. An avalanche goes straight over the top.

Trees are planted on slopes above villages, to protect the villages from avalanches.

Soldiers fire at slopes to start small avalanches and stop the snow from building up.

Conquering Everest

Everest is the highest mountain in the world. Many people had tried to climb it but had failed.

In March 1953 John Hunt and twelve friends went to Nepal to try and reach the summit.

They set up camp at the base of the mountain. They practised climbing for several weeks.

They hired local men to carry supplies. Their leader, Tenzing, was an experienced climber.

The climb was very dangerous. Sometimes they had to use ladders to cross crevasses.

The men climbed in groups, marking the way with flags in case snow later covered it.

There was a storm almost every day. It was very hard to walk because of strong winds.

The teams carried supplies up the mountain in relays. They set up camps along the way.

The night before they planned to climb to the top, there was a storm, which delayed them.

Tenzing and Hillary were chosen to climb the last peak. They ate a meal before starting.

They set off early in the morning. They were so high up, they had to wear oxygen masks.

When they reached the top, Hillary took photos to prove it. The date was May 23, 1953.

Volcanoes

A volcano may look like any other mountain. People live and farm on the lower slopes.

There is a crater at the top of a volcano. It often puffs out smoke and ashes.

Where the Earth's crust is thin, hot liquid rock can break through to form a volcano.

Sometimes there is a huge explosion. Hot rocks, ash and gases shoot from the volcano.

Red-hot, liquid rock, called lava, pours out of the crater. It flows downhill, covering anything in its way. As it cools, it hardens into rock and builds up the volcano.

This is a cast of a body trapped in the ashes of Vesuvius which buried the town of Pompeii in AD 79.

Volcanoes sometimes erupt in the sea. In 1963 one erupted off the coast of Iceland and made a new island. It is called Surtsey.

Scientists sometimes go down inside volcanoes to find out more about them. They wear special suits to protect them from the heat.

Mountains of the Moon

The Ruwenzori Mountains in Africa are called the Mountains of the Moon. They look mysterious and are often partly hidden in the clouds.

The peaks are always covered in snow, but it is hot all year round at the bottom. At different heights there are different plants and animals.

Chameleon

Above the grassy plains there is jungle. Even though it is hot, it rains nearly every day.

This small chameleon lives in the jungle. Local people think that it brings bad luck.

Steamy bamboo forests grow at the next level. Bamboo grows as much as a metre a day here.

There is a cold, wet heath above the bamboo forest. Thick moss grows underfoot and the dripping trees are covered in lichen.

Strange plants and giant, spikey flowers grow among the beds of mosses. Small birds and some animals live even at this height.

Higher up there is bare rock. It is too cold for most plants to grow here. The lake is filled by water running down from a glacier.

The Mountains of the Moon have six peaks which are usually covered in cloud. It is very cold up here and snows nearly every day.

Glaciers

Hollow full of snow

A glacier starts where snow heaps up on a slope high on a mountain. The snow packs together and turns to ice. The weight of any new snow then slowly pushes the ice downhill.

A glacier is a river of solid ice which creeps slowly down snow-covered mountains.

Climbing a glacier

The glacier only moves a few centimetres a day down the mountain.

Climbers often use glaciers as a short cut up a mountain. But ice falls and huge blocks of ice can make them difficult to climb.

Glaciers have a lot of dangerous deep cracks in them. These are called crevasses. Some crevasses are as much as 30 metres deep. They are often hidden by snow.

Crevasses

In winter glaciers are covered in snow. The snow makes bridges across crevasses.

The bridges look safe but can be dangerous. They may collapse under a climber.

Climbers must be rescued from crevasses quickly, before they freeze to death.

The end of the glacier is called the snout.

This car park is for tourists who have come to see the glacier.

These rocks and stones have been carried here by the glacier. They are called moraine.

Deep crevasses

A glacier carries along anything that falls on to it, such as rocks. A dead man once appeared at the end of a glacier. He had fallen into a crevasse almost 100 years before.

The glacier melts as it gets warmer lower down the mountain. Streams of meltwater from the end of the glacier run down to the valley.

Mountains of the World

There are many shapes of mountain. These pointed peaks in France are called the 'needles'.

Some mountains have flat tops, like the Table Mountain in Cape Town, South Africa.

Other mountains have rounded tops. This mountain in Brazil is called the Sugar Loaf.

There are mountains all over the world. Some are in deserts. Some mountain ranges are under the sea and the tops are islands.

There are even mountains near the South Pole. They do not look high because the ice there is so deep that only the peaks show through.

A lot of wood comes from mountain forests. Lumberjacks chop down trees, then grow new ones. These logs are being floated to a sawmill.

Some of the world's most useful metals and precious stones are found deep inside mountains. Miners dig tunnels to find them.

Dam

In many valleys, rivers have been dammed to make lakes. The water is piped to towns, or used to drive machines which make electricity.

Where the Mountains Are

Grizzly bears live in the mountains of North America.

Early settlers crossed the Rocky Mountains in covered waggons.

Llamas are used as pack animals in the Andes.

Machu Picchu is a very old fortress town in the Andes.

GREENLAND

ICELAND

Alaska Range ALASKA

Mount McKinley

NORTH AMERICA

Surtsey

The Alp

Rocky Mountains

The Pyrenees

Appalachian Mountains

Atlas Mountains

ATLANTIC OCEAN

Ahaggar Mountain

AFRIC

PACIFIC OCEAN

SOUTH AMERICA

The Andes — longest mountain range in the world

Mount Aconcagua

Table Mounta

Scandinavia

Ural Mountains

ASIA

OPE

Caucasus

USSR

Altai Mountains

CHINA

The Himalayas – world's highest mountain range

Fujiyama

JAPAN

Mount Everest

PACIFIC OCEAN

Ethiopian Highlands

Mountains of the Moon

Kilimanjaro

NEW GUINEA

INDIAN OCEAN

AUSTRALIA
Great Dividing Range

NEW ZEALAND

ANTARCTICA

Surtsey is an island made of volcanic lava.

Hillary and Tenzing were the first men to climb Everest.

The snow leopard lives in the Himalayas and Altai Mountains.

These grassy mountains are in China.

Many tribes live in the mountains of New Guinea.

Index

First published in 1980 by Usborne Publishing Ltd, Usborne House, 83-85 Saffron Hill, London, EC1N 8RT, England. Revised edition published 1990. Copyright © 1990, 1980 Usborne Publishing Ltd. All rights reserved. No part of this publication may be reproduced, stored in a retrieval system, or transmitted by any means, electronic, mechanical, photocopying, recording or otherwise, without the prior permission of the publisher. The name Usborne and the device 🎈 are the Trade Marks of Usborne Publishing Ltd.

Printed in Italy